CH   SEP 1 7 1996

Fundamental

Coach Lori Coleman and these Richfield athletes were photographed for this book:

Rachel Ekholm,
Mandy Engberg,
Nate Evans-Winkel,
Angelina Gearhart,
Casey Herbert,
Ernest Julean,
Kacie Larson,
Vas Leckas,
Nichole Legus,
Jennifer Lenberg,
Neil Lenzen,
Elizabeth Petrik,
Marissa Santos,
Niels Sorensen,
Erick Stevens,
Wendy Walstrom.

Fundamental
SOCCER

Lori Coleman

Photographs by Andy King

Lerner Publications Company ● Minneapolis

To Punky, whose excitement for each new day is my inspiration.

Library of Congress Cataloging-in-Publication Data

Coleman, Lori.
  Fundamental soccer / by Lori Coleman ; photographs by Andy King.
    p. cm. — (Fundamental sports)
  Includes bibliographical references and index.
  ISBN 0–8225–3451-7
  1. Soccer—Juvenile literature. [1. Soccer.] I. King, Andy, ill. II. Title. III. Series.
GV943.25.C65 1995
796.334—dc20   94–11907

Manufactured in the United States of America
2 3 4 5 6 7 – HP – 01 00 99 98 97 96

The Fundamental Sports series was conceptualized by editor Julie Jensen, designed by graphic artist Michael Tacheny, and composed on a Macintosh computer by Robert Mauzy.

Photo Acknowledgments
Photographs are reproduced with the permission of: pp. 7, 8 (both), The Bettman Archive; p. 9, Allsport/David Cannon; p. 27, ©Jon Van Woerden; p. 58, Mark Backlund/Courtesy of Corner Kick Indoor Soccer Center, Maplewood, Minn.

Contents

Chapter 1

How This Game Got Started

The excitement of a soccer match cannot be beaten. Soccer is one of the most popular sports in the world because it is a fast-moving game with lots of action. Two teams of 11 players move the ball around a large field with quick passes and hard kicks. Thundering shots on goal and narrow saves by leaping goalkeepers keep soccer fans on the edge of their seats.

The only thing more exciting than watching a soccer match is playing the game yourself. Soccer is, in fact, the world's most popular team game. More people play and watch soccer than any other team sport, including baseball, basketball, hockey, and American football. In the United States, 1.92 million athletes participate in youth soccer leagues. Soccer is the national sport of many countries in Europe, Asia, Africa, and South America.

This Greek sculpture from the fifth century shows an ancient soccer player practicing.

Early Romans were soccer players.

Soccer's origin is unclear, because games like it were played around the world in ancient times. Most historians agree, however, that a game similar to modern soccer was first played in Derby, England, around A.D. 217, when Romans occupied the country. The Romans probably passed along a game that they had started playing in earlier times. In England, it became known as football.

For centuries, the game continued to be popular. The ball could be advanced only with the feet, the torso, or the head. Hands could not be used. Then in 1823, another game—later called rugby—was invented. Rugby had different rules. Players could use their hands to catch and throw the ball.

This drawing shows an American soccer match in 1890.

The London Football Association was formed in protest against the way rugby players carried the ball. Association members wanted to continue playing with the original rules. The association called the original version of football "association football" to distinguish it from rugby. The name was shortened to "assoc" and later was changed to "soccer," although the English and other Europeans also continued to use the name football.

Soccer was the only football game in the United States until the 1870s, when American football first became popular. In 1913 the United States Football Association was formed to govern the sport of soccer. In 1945 the governing body became known as the United States Soccer Federation (USSF).

The USSF runs professional, amateur, and youth soccer programs. The USSF organizes and manages national teams that play teams from other countries. The organization also supervises college-level play, Olympic teams, and a number of other specialty programs.

The Federation Internationale de Football Association (FIFA) governs soccer at the international level. More than 158 nations belong to FIFA. Most soccer games, including those played in the United States, are played by FIFA rules.

FIFA holds a very popular tournament every four years, called the World Cup. All member nations can compete to become one of the top 24 teams, which play in the tournament. Although the World Cup has not always caused a lot of excitement in the United States, it is the ultimate sporting event for people

In the 1990 World Cup Final, West Germany delighted its fans by defeating Argentina 1–0.

in many other countries. During some World Cup competitions, businesses and factories around the world have closed so that workers could watch the games. Fans parade in the streets. Mobs go crazy.

Soccer is not as popular in the United States as it is in other countries. Several professional leagues have started in America and then folded because not enough sports fans supported them. But many people are working to increase soccer's popularity. American soccer fans were thrilled that the World Cup games were held in the United States in 1994. More than 3.5 million people, some from other countries, attended the 52 games. Brazil defeated Italy in the final, 3–2, after a penalty kick shootout.

Chapter 2

BASICS

Field of Play

A soccer field is always a large rectangle, but it can be from 100 to 130 yards long and from 50 to 100 yards wide. Young players often use smaller fields, while more experienced teams play on larger fields.

A **center line** divides the field in half, and a **center spot** directly in the middle of the field is encircled by the **center circle**. The center spot is where the ball is first put in play to start a game.

A **goal** 8 yards wide and 8 feet high stands at each end of the field. A netting is stretched between two **goalposts** on the sides and a **crossbar** across the top. Players try to kick the soccer ball into the opposing team's goal. When they are able to do this, their team scores a point. Around the **goal area** is a larger **penalty area**, which extends 18 yards out from the goal. Within the penalty area lies the **penalty spot**. The **corner areas** and **penalty arcs** also are marked. These markings are important when a soccer rule has been broken.

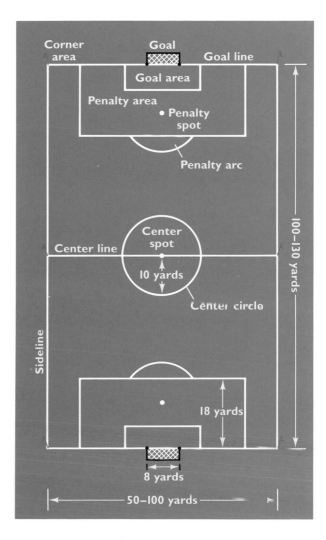

Corner area • Goal • Goal line • Goal area • Penalty area • Penalty spot • Penalty arc • Center spot • 10 yards • Center circle • Center line • Sideline • 18 yards • 8 yards • 50–100 yards • 100–130 yards

11

Equipment

Soccer shoes are very important and should be chosen with care to make sure they fit correctly. Shoes that fit poorly can affect a player's performance and can even cause injury. Soccer shoes worn for regular outdoor play have rubber or plastic cleats. The cleats

dig into the ground and provide the players with firm footing.

Soccer players usually wear T-shirts for practice and jerseys for games. Loose shorts and long socks make up the rest of the uniform. In games, players wear shin guards and mouth guards to prevent injuries.

The **goalkeeper** stays by his or her team's goal and tries to prevent balls from entering it. The goalkeeper (goalie, for short) wears gloves and a uniform with extra padding. The goalkeeper's uniform must be a color different from that of his or her teammates' uniforms so that opponents can easily tell which player is the one allowed to use his or her hands.

Balls

Sporting goods shops sell soccer balls in many colors and designs. Balls range in price, depending on the brand, material, and quality. Leather balls are best, but balls made from rubber or nylon also are available. Hand-sewn leather balls are softer and last longer than balls made from rubber or nylon, but the synthetic balls are cheaper.

The official size of a soccer ball is 27 to 28 inches around and 14 to 16 ounces in weight. Younger players sometimes play with smaller balls that weigh less and are easier to kick.

Basic Moves

The Richfield Football Club practices basic soccer moves every day. The most important skills to master include dribbling, passing, trapping, shooting, heading, and defending.

Dribbling

Soccer players move the ball on the field by **dribbling** the ball with their feet. Running while controlling the ball with your feet takes lots of practice.

To improve, Kacie and her teammates dribble while jogging. With each step, Kacie touches the ball with either the laces or outside of her foot. She uses both her left foot and her right foot to dribble. After the players are comfortable making these touches with their feet, they practice dribbling while sprinting, changing speeds, and changing directions.

It's important to practice changing speeds and directions while dribbling, because these skills help you maintain possession of the ball during a game. A good way to get away from an opponent challenging you for the ball is to use a fake.

With the ball close by and under control, Nate keeps his body between his opponent and the ball. To get away from the other player he lunges his body in one direction so that his opponent also moves that way. Then he touches the ball with the bottom of his foot, rolling it in the opposite direction. He quickly takes off dribbling in the opposite direction of his fake.

Inside of foot

Outside of foot

Instep of foot

Passing

Jessica and Kristy are **passing** the ball back and forth. Because passing is the quickest and surest way to move the ball, accurate passes on the field are important for good team play. Players often stop the ball before passing it to a teammate.

First, they pass with the inside of their feet. This is the safest pass because it is very accurate when done correctly. Jessica places her nonkicking foot next to the ball. The ankle of her kicking foot must be held firmly for a crisp pass. After she hits the ball, her leg follows through, giving power to the pass.

Next, Jessica demonstrates a pass with the outside of her foot. This time, the nonkicking foot is placed far enough from the ball to give the kicking foot room to swing. Jessica makes sure she keeps her ankles firm and follows through.

Kacie and her teammates are practicing long passes. For a more powerful kick to send the ball a longer distance, Kacie passes with her **instep,** hitting the ball with the laces of her shoe.

The heel of the foot is used to make a quick pass to a teammate behind you. Rachel demonstrates the **heel pass**, placing her nonkicking foot next to the ball and swinging back with her kicking foot. Her heel sends the ball to Alex behind her.

Sometimes in a game there isn't time to stop the ball before passing it to a teammate. To receive a ball and pass it all in the same motion, players use the **one-touch pass**. As the ball reaches Rachel, she positions herself directly in its path and swings her kicking foot to connect with the ball as it reaches her, sending it in the direction she wants to pass.

When the ball is in the air, the one-touch pass is called **a volley pass**. Again, Rachel positions herself in the ball's path and swings her leg to meet the ball with her foot.

Trapping

Along with passing, the Reds practice **trapping** the ball. Trapping is stopping the ball with your body and then putting the ball in position to pass or dribble it. To receive a pass, players often need to trap the ball and control it before continuing play.

You can trap a ball with your foot, thigh, abdomen, or chest. Kacie traps ground balls with her foot. Lifting her foot off the ground, she meets the ball with the inside of that foot and lets her leg move back a little bit to soften the impact.

Low air balls also can be trapped with the foot. When the ball is bouncing or traveling in the air just over the ground, it can be stopped using the instep. Holding her foot out, with the ankle firm, Kacie traps the ball on the laces of her shoe. Upon impact, she draws her foot back a little so that the ball does not bounce off her foot and out of her reach. As she softens the impact, the ball drops on the ground in front of her.

Kacie traps higher balls with her body. When the ball is in the air, she positions herself where the ball will come down. Before it bounces on the ground, she meets it with her thigh, drawing back her leg when the ball hits to soften the impact.

Next, Kacie traps a high ball by jumping up to meet it with her abdomen. As the ball hits, she gathers it in by leaning into the ball with her body.

To trap even higher balls, players use their chests. With the **chest trap**, Kristy can control where the ball will fall by turning her body when the ball hits. As the ball reaches her, she gets in front of it and uses her upper chest as a table on which the ball can land. As it hits, she leans her body forward and to the left so that the ball falls in that direction.

Shooting

Shooting, like passing, requires accuracy. But shooting also calls for a very powerful kick. Mandy practices taking hard shots at the goal, using the instep to gain the most power.

Running up to the ball, Mandy places her nonkicking foot next to the ball and strikes the ball with the laces of her kicking foot. As Mandy shoots, she concentrates on keeping her ankle rigid and following through with her swinging leg. After the shot, Mandy lands on her kicking foot.

Like passing, shooting can be done using either foot. Players also can shoot with the outside of the foot. But most soccer players prefer shooting with the instep of their strongest leg and they practice their best shot over and over.

Some young players have trouble getting their foot underneath the ball to lift it into the air. Practice this by concentrating on hitting the ball with the correct part of the foot and then following through.

Heading

Casey is also trying to score goals, but instead of shooting, she is practicing **headers**—hitting the ball with her head at the hairline. Soccer players can use the heading technique to send the ball downfield, to pass to a teammate, or to put the ball in the goal.

To properly head the ball, Casey watches the ball and positions herself where the ball will land. With her arms out in front of her, Casey moves to the ball with her whole body. Upon impact, she brings her shoulders forward, swings her arms back, keeps her neck and chin firm, and keeps her eyes open. Casey hits the ball with her upper forehead, right at her hairline.

When heading the ball, be confident. Headers do not hurt when they are done correctly. Remember, you are hitting the ball instead of letting the ball hit you.

Defense

Defense is what you do when your team does not have the ball. All players must play defense for a team to succeed. An important defensive skill is **marking**.

Marking

To mark her opponent, Marissa keeps close to the player while staying between that player and the goal that Marissa's team is defending. If the player that Marissa is marking has the ball, Marissa tries to force that player to take the ball where Marissa wants it to go. For example, if Marissa does not want the player to take a shot at the goal, she forces her opponent to the sideline and out of bounds.

Tackling

To play defense, soccer players also must be able to challenge and **tackle**, or take the ball out of an opponent's control. While marking a player on the opposing team, Marissa forces the player with the ball to stop and make a turn. Marissa makes a move to take away the ball and gains possession.

Goalkeeping

In addition to all the basic moves, goalkeepers need to learn another set of skills important for their special role on the field. The goalkeeper is the only player allowed to use his or her hands to play the ball (except when a player is throwing in the ball from the sidelines).

The goalie has to be ready to quickly move in any direction. From the **basic stance,** the goalkeeper can reach, leap, and dive quickly. With his or her knees slightly bent, the goalkeeper stands with his or her feet about shoulder-width apart. The goalie's arms and hands are raised and ready to stop any shot at the goal. Shots that would go in the goal if the goalkeeper didn't intercept them are called **shots on goal**.

Positioning

Positioning is a technique used by goalkeepers to minimize the goal area open to the opposing shooter. By moving off the goal line into the field, the goalkeeper makes the open goal space look smaller to the shooter. The goalkeeper then can judge more easily where the shot will be aimed and block it.

Collecting

The most important part of goalkeeping is **collecting** balls. Goalkeepers have to collect, or save, many shots on goal—rolling balls, bouncing balls, and high balls.

To pick up rolling balls, Nichole keeps her feet close enough together that the ball cannot fit through them. Leaning over, she holds her hands out and slightly apart with the palms up. As Nichole picks up the ball, she scoops it up to her chest with her arms.

Keeper ! ! !

Tony Meola is probably the best goalkeeper from the United States. Meola grew up in Kearny, New Jersey. Meola and other young people in Kearny grew up watching the New York Cosmos, a pro team that played in the now-defunct North American Soccer League. Meola's family is from Italy, and the young goalkeeper hopes to play there professionally.

Meola's childhood involved baseball as well as soccer. In high school, he was an all-state baseball player as well as an all-state soccer player. With the opportunity to continue on in either sport, Meola chose soccer. He went on to play at the University of Virginia. Later he joined the United States Soccer Federation and helped the U.S. team compete in the 1994 World Cup.

Meola, known as "Meat" or "Meatball" by his teammates, has earned his reputation as a tough keeper not for narrow, diving saves or for spectacular ball punches. He is effective in goal because of his ability to control situations and affect plays before his opponents know what is happening. Meola often comes off the line and destroys an attack by intercepting a pass or stealing the ball from a dribbler. He can beat almost anyone in the air, and he can punt the ball more than 80 yards downfield. Meola is a keeper to watch in world-class soccer.

When catching balls in the air, Elizabeth positions herself so that her body is between the shot and the goal. She holds her hands with the palms out and her thumbs together so that her hands form a W. Upon impact, Elizabeth brings the ball in to her body.

To save high balls, the goalkeeper must jump up to reach them. Elizabeth anticipates a shot at the upper right corner of the goal. As the shot is taken, Elizabeth gets into position and leaps on one leg, bringing the other knee up as she extends her arms to catch the ball in midair.

Sometimes the goalie will be unable to reach a fast-moving shot quickly enough to catch it. In order to make a save, the goalkeeper may have to deflect the ball up over the goal or off to one side. With her wrist and hand held firmly, Nichole jumps up on one leg and punches the ball up and over the net with a short, quick stroke.

Diving

Some of the most exciting saves that goalkeepers make are done by **diving**. Diving is difficult and takes a lot of practice. When training, many goal-

keepers begin by diving from a kneeling position. Rachel positions herself on her knees while a teammate tosses the ball to each side. As the ball approaches, Rachel reaches out, keeping the lower hand directly in the line of the ball's flight. The upper hand is placed on top of the ball as it hits.

Next Elizabeth demonstrates diving from the basic stance position. As she takes off from the basic stance, Elizabeth extends her arms. Upon impact, she gathers in the ball and gets ready to hit the ground. Elizabeth rolls as she hits the ground to soften her fall and immediately gets up to see where her team-mates are before she returns the ball to the playing field.

Once the goalkeeper has made a save, he or she must put the ball back into play. To pass the ball to a nearby teammate, the goalkeeper often throws the ball. To be successful, these passes must be accurate.

To send the ball a longer distance down the field, the goalkeeper **punts**. The best punts are hard kicks that send the ball flying far, but low to the ground. High-flying balls give the opposing team more time to react, and the power of the kick is wasted in giving the ball height instead of distance. Elizabeth holds the ball and takes a couple of steps to build up her momentum and give her kick power. Holding the ball over her kicking foot, Elizabeth swings her leg and kicks through the ball.

Chapter 3

GAME TIME

Positions

In the game of soccer, there are 11 players on a team. One of the 11 is the goalkeeper, and the other 10 are in one of three basic positions: forward, full-back, and midfield.

Forwards generally score the goals, but they have a lot of work to do before getting a chance to take a shot on goal. Forwards move to open spaces, make good passes, support teammates with the ball, and dribble past defenders to get into a position where they can shoot. Forwards positioned on the outside, near the sidelines, are called **wings**.

Fullbacks are the last line of defense in front of the goalkeeper. They mark players on the opposing team and try to force them to make a bad pass or dribble. Fullbacks keep opponents out of the area in front of the goal. They work together and cover for each other when one gets pulled out of position by the opponent he or she is marking.

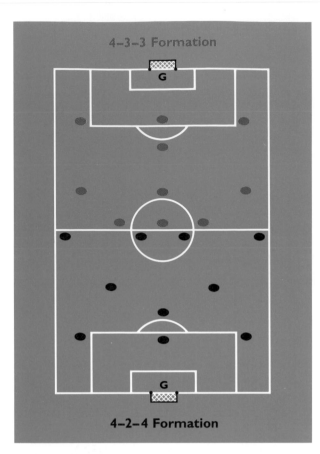

4–3–3 Formation

4–2–4 Formation

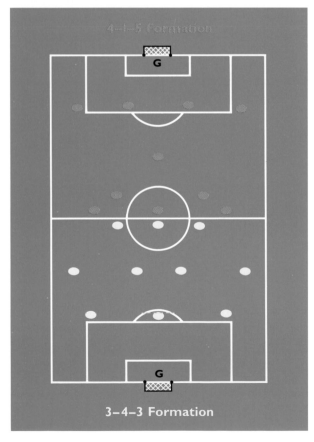

4–1–5 Formation

3–4–3 Formation

Midfielders play both offense and defense. They help the forwards bring the ball down the field and into scoring position. They also hustle back to help the fullbacks defend the goal.

Coaches use many formations of forwards, midfielders, and defenders. Some of the most common formations are shown.

Rules

A goal is scored when the entire ball crosses the goal line between the goalposts and under the crossbar. Each goal scored is one point. Depending on the league, ties are broken either by overtime periods or by shootouts.

Soccer games usually have two equal periods of playing time. Playing time can vary from 30-minute halves for youth games to 45-minute halves for upper-level leagues.

Play begins with the **kickoff** at the center spot. A coin toss before the game determines which team will kick off. The team that does not kick off at the beginning of the game will kick off at the start of the second period. After a team scores a goal, a player from the other team kicks off. The players on the team that is not kicking off cannot be in the center circle until one player from the kicking team has kicked the ball. The ball must rotate one full turn before it is in play and another player can touch it.

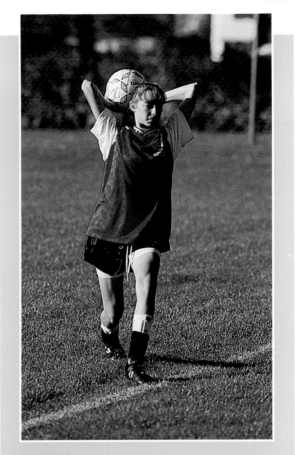

The entire ball must cross the sideline or the goal line for the ball to be out of bounds. When the ball goes out of bounds, it is out of play and must be returned to the field for play to resume. If the ball goes out over a sideline, the team that did not send the ball out is awarded a **throw-in**. When the referee awards a team a throw-in, a player from that team throws the ball back into play. The thrower must stand outside of the sideline with both feet on the ground. The thrower must use both hands, throwing the ball from directly over his or her head, to make the throw.

If the ball goes out of bounds over the goal line and the team defending the goal last touched it, the opposing team is given a **corner kick**. The corner kick is made from one of the two corner areas on the end of the field where the ball went out of bounds. A player can score on a corner kick alone, but usually the ball is kicked to the area in front of the goal for a teammate to shoot or head into the net.

When the ball goes out over the goal line and the team defending the goal did not touch it last, that team is given a **goal kick**. For a goal kick, the ball is placed in the goal area, usually on the corner. The person taking the goal kick should be able to kick the ball far down the field from a stationary position.

Throw-ins

In soccer, the only time players other than the goalie can play the ball with their hands is to do a throw-in. When a team is awarded a **throw-in,** the defender or the midfielder playing on the side of the field where the ball went out usually throws.

Standing a short distance from the sideline, the thrower watches the movement on the field to see which teammate may be open to field the ball. The thrower's hands are wrapped around the ball with the thumbs touching. To throw, the player brings the ball up over his or her head while stepping forward. The second step adds momentum, and with the third step, the player throws the ball.

Both feet must be on the ground and on or behind the sideline when the ball is thrown. The ball must be thrown directly over the player's head. If the player makes an improper throw-in, the opposing team is awarded a throw-in at the same place.

Yellow Card, Red Card

In a soccer game, the referee makes the call regarding a foul or restart situation (after the ball has gone out of play). Players must respect the referee and abide by the calls the referee makes.

*If a referee believes that a player is arguing, using foul language, or harassing an official or another player, he or she may show the player a **yellow card**. The yellow card is a caution to the player that any other misconduct will be met with a **red card**. A red card means that player is expelled from the game. Other actions that can result in a caution or ejection from the game include entering the game without the referee's permission, violent behavior, and wasting time.*

Drop Ball

*If the referee has to stop play—for instance, if a player is injured or ill—the game is restarted with a **drop ball**. Drop balls are sometimes also called when the ball goes out of bounds and the referee did not see which team last touched it. A drop ball takes place at the spot where the ball was last in play.*

In a drop ball, one player from each team stands near the referee. The referee blows the whistle, drops the ball between the two players, and play begins.

Fouls

In a soccer game, the referee decides when the rules have been broken. Some violations of the rules are considered **major violations**. These include pushing, tripping, holding, and **handball**. The referee calls handball if a player other than the goalkeeper uses his or her hands or arms to play the ball.

Minor violations of the rules include being **offside**. A player is offside if he or she is ahead of the ball in the attacking half of the field without at least two opponents between him or her and the goal. Offside is not called in corner kick, goal kick, or throw-in situations.

Other minor violations include **dangerous play** and **obstruction**. An example of dangerous play is a high kick that could injure another player. Obstruction is intentionally blocking an opponent rather than going for the ball.

If the referee calls a major violation, a **direct free kick** is awarded to the team that did not commit the foul. For minor violations, the opposing team is awarded an **indirect free kick**. Direct and indirect free kicks are taken from the spot where the violation occurred. All players must stand at least 10 yards away from the spot where the ball is placed. A direct free kick can score a goal. A second player must touch the ball after an indirect free kick before it goes into the net.

If a major violation occurs within a team's penalty area, the opponents are awarded a **penalty kick**. The penalty kick is taken from the penalty spot, only 12 yards from the goal line. Only the goalie can defend the goal, so more often than not a goal is scored!

Playing the Game

The Richfield Reds and the Richfield Wildcats—teams in the city's football club—always start off the season by playing against each other. The Wildcats won the coin toss, so they have the kickoff. Before they go out to their positions on the field, the Wildcats gather in a huddle for a cheer.

Two forwards, Becky and Laura, make the first play of the game. Laura kicks the ball forward from the center spot, and Becky makes a long pass out to the wing. Melissa carries the ball down the line until the fullback challenges her and comes up with the ball. The Reds player sends the ball down to the Wildcats' half of the field. The Wildcats hustle back to play defense.

When the Reds' right forward dribbles down toward the Wildcats' goal, Chinda comes up to tackle for the ball. As she does, Marissa—who is playing center fullback—moves over to cover Chinda's territory. After the ball is played out of bounds, Chinda moves back into position as left fullback, and Marissa shifts back over to the center. By working together this way, the Wildcats can keep their opponents from scoring.

After about 15 minutes, some of the Wildcats are getting tired. Coach Casas calls for a substitution when the Wildcats have a goal kick. A coach can make substitutions on the field when his or her team has a goal kick or a throw-in. Angelina and Xanara come onto the field to relieve two of the midfielders.

Jenny takes the goal kick, sending the ball downfield to Kacie. Kacie turns with the ball and sees an opponent coming right at her. Kacie fakes that

Special Tips

The quickest way to move the ball around the field is by passing. Teams that pass well are successful because the players stay spread out over the field without bunching. If two or three players are in the same spot and one of them gains possession of the ball, the other two won't be in position to receive a pass. And two or three teammates bunched in one place means many open spaces on the field where the opposing team's players have no competition for the ball. By keeping distance between you and your teammates, you will be better at passing and receiving passes.

Soccer players need to be aware of where their teammates and opponents are at all times. The ball can move in the blink of an eye, and if you get the ball but weren't paying attention, you may not know of a nearby opponent who could steal the ball. If you do not know where your teammates are, you won't know where to pass the ball.

she is going to the left and takes the ball to the right, past the other player! She dribbles and then passes to Xanara. Xanara looks up and sees several Reds in front of her, so she passes back to Angelina and makes a break, sprinting downfield to an open spot. Angelina makes a one-touch pass—called a **wall pass**—back to Xanara and Xanara continues dribbling toward the Reds' goal. As she approaches the goal line, Xanara turns and makes a long, high kick right in front of the goal. Kacie jumps up and heads the ball toward the goal. She scores!

Now the Reds start with the ball. Before the Wildcats' defense has a chance to get ready, the Reds pass the ball several times, and one of the players takes a shot on goal. Nichole is ready for the high shot and jumps up to grab it. As she punts the ball back down the field, the Wildcats' defense is moving in that direction. Katie yells, "I got it!" and traps the ball with her stomach. She can't turn, because a Red is in her way. Katie passes the ball back—a **support pass**—and Emily sends the ball across the field to the left side, where Wildcats are open.

All too soon, the referee blows his whistle. Halftime is called. Coach Casas talks to the Wildcats about the first half. They are only ahead by one point. Coach Casas reminds the players to keep spread out on the field. Many times, two or three players go for the ball, creating a crowded situation and leaving no one open to take a pass. "Make sure you talk to each other and call for balls and for passes," the coach reminds them.

Both teams are ready for the second half. Soon after it begins, Angelina gets the ball near the middle of the field. Becky makes a break and sprints toward the Reds' goal, ready for a pass. Angelina passes the ball to Becky up in front, and the referee blows his whistle. "Watch offside!" yells Coach Casas. Becky had moved past all of the defenders, leaving just the goalkeeper between her and the goal before she received the pass. The Reds get a free kick.

Later in the game, Angelina plays another ball downfield to Becky. This time, a Red defender and the goalkeeper are between Becky and the goal. Becky sprints downfield with the ball and the defender runs up to meet her. Becky stops the ball and fakes a shot. The defender moves to block the shot and Becky dribbles the ball around her. Now it is between Becky and the Reds' goalkeeper. The goalkeeper comes off the goal line and starts toward Becky. Becky aims and shoots the ball to the lower right corner—another score!

The Reds rush to start the ball in play again. Now the Reds are two goals down, and they need to score soon to have a chance at winning. The Reds quickly bring the ball toward the Wild-

cats' goal. Trying to keep the ball out of the dangerous penalty area, Marissa accidentally kicks the ball out past the goal line. The Reds get a corner kick. The Wildcats' defense marks up Reds in front of the goal. The corner kick is a high ball right in front of the goal. A Red forward meets the ball in the air with her foot, volleying it right past Nichole into the goal. The Reds have a point.

The Wildcats start the ball in the center. Players on both teams are getting tired, but they play hard because either team could still win. But sooner than they expect it, the referee blows his whistle one last time. The game is over. The Wildcats win!

It was a close game and both teams played well. The Reds and Wildcats line up and shake hands.

Total Soccer

All players attack and all players defend in total soccer. Teams that succeed at total soccer have players who are able to fill in at one another's positions and can play defense or offense. For example, a forward may see that a fullback on her team is challenging an opposing player for the ball. Instead of standing upfield, the forward hustles back to cover at defense in case the fullback gets beat.

Players can switch positions on offense as well. If a fullback has possession of the ball and sees that his best option is to carry the ball upfield instead of passing, he does so—knowing that a teammate will cover his position until he gets back.

Advanced teams that have played together for a long time can excel at total soccer because the teammates are familiar with one another's skills and playing styles.

Chapter 4

PRACTICE, PRACTICE

Richfield boys and girls teams practice on the days they don't play games. Each practice session includes some stretching, running, and drills.

Conditioning

After the boys have dribbled around the soccer field to warm up their muscles, they get into a circle for stretching. First they stretch all the muscles in their legs. Then they stretch their backs, arms, and necks.

After stretching, team captains Niels and Neil lead the players in some warm-up exercises. Neil demonstrates the first exercise: jumping over the ball. With his feet close together, Neil stands next to the ball. He jumps over the ball, keeping his feet together, and lands on the other side of the ball. He and his teammates do this 25 times.

Next, Neil demonstrates the same exercise, but jumps over the ball forward and backward. The Reds do this 25 times, too. These exercises help the Reds improve their coordination and increase their leg strength.

Now the boys are doing exercises to strengthen their stomach muscles. Each player gets a partner and links ankles with the partner while in sit-up position. The partners pass a soccer ball back and forth as they do sit-ups, and the one with the ball must touch it to the ground behind his head as he finishes the sit-up.

In the next exercise, each player lies on the ground with a soccer ball between his feet. When the coach yells "Six inches!" they lift their feet up six inches off the ground, still holding the ball between them. Then the coach yells "Up!" and the players slowly raise their feet up even more, until the ball is directly overhead.

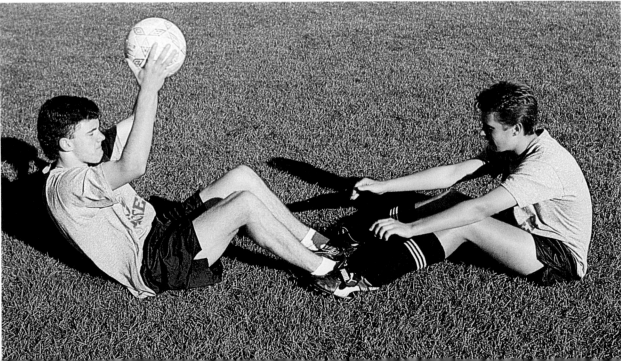

Erick demonstrates another exercise, which is a favorite. First, Erick throws the ball up in the air, as high and as straight up as possible. After throwing the ball, Erick quickly leaps into a somersault, bounds back up, and tries to catch the ball. The first time, Erick is too late and jumps up to see the ball bounce next to him. But on the next try, he finishes the somersault and has plenty of time to catch the ball in midair.

The Reds want to increase their speed and their stamina. Sprinting helps make them faster. Jogging helps build up their endurance. One exercise uses both jogging and sprinting. The boys line up and begin jogging around the field in single file. The last one in the line sprints to the front of the line, while everyone else is jogging, and yells for the next person to go. Again, the last one in line sprints to the front and the exercise continues.

In addition to running, soccer players do weight training to increase their strength. Once a week, the Reds boys and girls meet in the weight room at their school, where a weight trainer helps them with the equipment. Lifting weights makes the players' muscles stronger and less likely to be injured.

Drills and Skills Training

One of the most basic drills that soccer players can do to improve their game is **juggling**. Juggling improves ball-handling skills and can be done any time, since all a player needs is a ball.

Niels demonstrates juggling. The idea is to keep the ball from touching the ground, using touches with the feet, the thighs, the head, and any other part of the body except the hands and arms. The boys all try juggling, keeping track of the number of touches they get in before the ball bounces on the ground.

Dribbling drills are also a good way to improve ball-handling skills. For one drill, Coach Smith sets up a line of cones a couple of steps apart from one another. Starting at the first cone, Neil dribbles forward and weaves the ball around each of the cones. When he reaches the last cone, he quickly turns the ball and weaves back through to the starting line.

In another drill, each player gets a ball and stands inside the center circle on the field. When the coach blows his whistle, everyone begins to dribble around the circle, keeping their heads up so that they don't run into each other. Coach Smith calls out different touches that the players must do and then continue dribbling. When he calls "Inside!" the players make two quick touches with the inside of the foot and then sprint with the ball for a couple of steps before resuming a jogging dribble. When he calls "Outside!" they do the same with the outside of the foot. Coach Smith yells out "Touch!" and the boys touch the balls with the bottom of the foot before going on. And when he yells "Switch!" they quickly change direction.

After about 10 minutes, Coach Smith changes the drill slightly. Now, instead of calling a touch to be performed, he will raise his hand, holding up fingers. The Reds must all yell out how many fingers he is holding up. This drill helps the players get used to dribbling the ball without always looking at it.

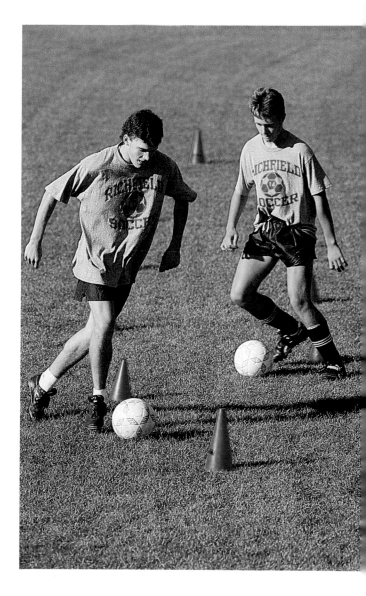

Next, the girls do the pass weave. Rachel, Jenny, and Wendy begin, standing side by side about 10 yards apart. Rachel has the ball in the middle. The three start jogging forward, and Rachel passes the ball out to Jenny to the right. Rachel then follows her pass and takes Jenny's place as Jenny takes a couple of dribbles toward the center. As they all constantly move forward, Jenny passes to Wendy and goes to the left. Wendy brings the ball to the center and passes to Rachel. They continue to the end of the field.

In another passing drill, one defender is in the middle of a circle of passers. Everyone in the circle passes the ball around, while the player in the middle tries to block a pass and get the ball. When he is successful, he takes the place of the player whose pass he blocked and that player goes in the middle.

A good way to practice skills against another player is one-on-one play. For this, the players get into pairs. Niels and Neil demonstrate the first one-on-one drill: shadowing. In this drill, one player has the ball and the other player simply marks him. Niels starts with the ball, and Neil follows him closely from behind. Neil does not try to take the ball away from Niels, but he tries to make it difficult for Niels to dribble in the direction he wants to go.

Next, Niels and Neil play one-on-one with two cones set up as goals. Each player tries to score by hitting the other person's cone with the ball. One-on-one play helps players learn how to move the ball around an opponent.

Another way to practice one-on-one play is to set up challenge situations in front of a regulation goal. With their goalkeeper in goal, the rest of the players line up in one of two lines—one at the edge of the goal and one at the top of the goal area. Each player behind the

endline has a ball. The first player in line passes the ball to the first person in the other line. That player must trap the ball and dribble in to try to shoot and score a goal. The other player speeds out to play defense against the attacker.

Playing with a smaller number of players is another good way to improve game skills. Six players on a team, three players against one player, four players on two players, or almost any variation will give players a chance to refine their passing and defending techniques.

RAZZLE DAZZLE

Even excellent soccer players need a lot of practice to stay in shape and to develop their abilities. With more and more practice, soccer players can play more skillfully. And the more a team plays together, the better teammates become at passing and playing together.

Practice also helps soccer players develop and perform more difficult moves. The better a player's ball-handling skills, the more he or she will be able to dribble past opponents in a game. For example, a good juggler will be able to use those juggling skills on the field by keeping the ball in possession while moving toward the goal. And good ball handlers have learned to be creative in their dribbling, using a variety of moves to go in any direction—not just forward. The best players use the width of the field and are not afraid to dribble out to the sideline or to pass the ball back to a teammate in a support position.

Pro Soccer in the United States

Professional soccer leagues have come and gone in the United States, as teams have lost players to foreign clubs and American fans have shown little interest in keeping professional soccer afloat. Many American players would like to be able to play at home instead of traveling to Europe and beyond to earn a living in the sport.

The United States Interregional Soccer League (USISL) began in 1986. In 1994 the USISL began the season with 43 teams— some semi-professional teams and some professional teams. Nationwide competition, organizers and coaches hope, will help increase the public's interest in the sport. Many of the league's teams give aspiring professionals experience with top-level play. Eventually, as players and their teams gain experience, the league plans to split into two divisions—an amateur and a professional—and foster competition with top-rated international teams.

Diving Header

When we watch advanced and professional soccer players in competitive
matches, we usually see a number of
spectacular moves that are performed
to outsmart and beat the opponent as
well as to impress the fans. One of these
is the **diving header**. Diving headers are
usually shots on goal, although at other
times they may be used to send the ball
downfield when under pressure. The ad-
vantage of diving to head the ball is that
you can quickly get to a ball and send it
with power. To practice diving headers,
players often start out in a sand pit for a
soft landing, until they have learned how
to land.

Vas and Nate are practicing diving
headers into the net. Vas tosses the ball
in front of Nate as he runs to the goal.
Nate dives forward, with his arms out to
the sides, and hits the ball with his forehead, keeping his neck firm and his
eyes open. Nate lands arms first on the
ground to soften the impact. Then it is
Vas's turn.

Sliding Tackle

Another breathtaking move is the **sliding tackle**. When an opponent breaks away to the goal with the ball, a defender may have little time to get in place. To gain possession of the ball quickly and effectively, he or she may slide tackle.

Running up to the play, Casey makes sure she concentrates on the ball. A slide tackle performed incorrectly can injure the other player and earn you a foul. When she is close to the ball, Casey tucks her right leg under and thrusts her left leg out as she slides for the ball. Just before the opponent gets a foot on it, Casey touches the ball, sending it out of her opponent's reach. Casey quickly gets up and recovers the ball.

Scissors Kick

The **scissors kick,** or **bicycle kick,** is done by jumping up in a backward somersault motion. In the air, as the kicking foot rises to strike the ball overhead, the nonkicking foot is thrust back and down to provide leverage and to give power to the kick. After making contact with the ball, Nate lands on the ground back first, cushioning his fall with his arms.

Indoors

Indoor soccer differs from regulation soccer mainly in the size of the field. An indoor field is much smaller—52 yards long and 36 yards wide. The goals are 12 feet wide and 6½ feet high. With a smaller playing space, indoor soccer uses fewer players. Each team has six players, including the goalkeeper, on the field at a time.

For indoor soccer, players wear rubber-soled shoes without cleats. Unlike grassy outdoor fields, indoor playing spaces have hard surfaces. For this reason, some players also choose to wear long pants instead of shorts.

When the ball passes over a sideline and out of bounds, the team that did not last touch it is awarded a **kick-in**. A player sets the ball on the sideline at the point where it crossed and kicks it in any direction back into play.

If the ball goes out of play across the goal line, and the defending team last touched it, the attacking team is awarded a corner kick. One of the players places the ball on the corner, where

the sideline and the goal line intersect, and kicks the ball into play. If the attacking team last touched the ball before it crossed the goal line, the defending team is given the ball. The goalkeeper must throw the ball back into play, but the ball cannot cross the center line. In fact, the goalkeeper can never throw, punt, or drop-kick the ball past the halfway line in indoor soccer. If the goalkeeper does play the ball past the center line, the opposing team is awarded an indirect free kick from the center line.

Although indoor soccer uses the same skills, the game is a bit different from soccer played on a larger field. With less room, players must think and react faster. Big, powerful kicks tend to send the ball out of bounds more often than not. Short, quick, accurate passes and good ball control will help a team win. Shots on goal should be kept low to the ground.

In northern areas of the United States, indoor soccer is popular because it can be played year-round.

SOCCER TALK

basic stance: The standing position from which a player—especially a goalkeeper—can most easily make a move for the ball. In the basic stance, the goalkeeper is on the toes, with the knees slightly bent and the arms out.

bicycle kick: An aerial kick done while jumping up and backwards in a back somersault motion. Also called a **scissors kick**.

center circle: The circle at the center of the field with a radius of 10 yards from the center spot.

center line: The line through the middle of the field that divides the field in half.

center spot: The spot in the center of the field from which kickoffs are taken.

chest trap: The technique of stopping a ball in the air by using the chest.

collecting: The technique of receiving a ground or airborne ball and controlling it before putting it in play. Also called trapping.

corner area: The arc around each of the field's four corners. Corner kicks are taken from these areas.

corner kick: A direct free kick taken from the corner area after the ball is played out of bounds past the goal line by the defending team.

crossbar: A bar, 8 yards long, that forms the top boundary of the goal and to which the net is attached.

dangerous play: A minor violation, such as a high kick, that could cause injury to another player.

defense: The type of play used when the ball is on a team's own side of the field. On defense, players work to move the ball away from their own goal.

direct free kick: A free kick that can score a goal without the ball being touched first by another player. A direct free kick is awarded to a team when the opposing team commits a major violation, such as handball.

diving: A technique used mainly by goalkeepers in an attempt to save a shot on goal.

diving header: A way to hit the ball powerfully with the head. The diving header is an advanced move.

dribbling: Running while touching the ball with the feet to keep it in control and moving along with the player.

forward: A player position, mainly used for offense. Forwards are usually goal scorers.

fullback: A player position, mainly used for defense. Fullbacks work with the goalkeeper to keep the opposing team from shooting on goal and scoring.

goal: The area between the goalposts and the crossbar. A team scores a point when the ball is completely inside the opponents' goal.

goalposts: The two bars, both 8 feet tall, that define the boundaries of the goal and to which the crossbar and netting are attached.

handball: The use of the hands by anyone other than the goalkeeper to play the ball. Handball is a major violation.

header: A technique used to play the ball by hitting it with the forehead, near the hairline.

heel pass: A way to pass the ball back to a player in a support position. Instead of turning, the passer stops the ball and hits it back with the heel.

indirect free kick: A free kick that cannot score a goal without first touching another player. Indirect free kicks are awarded when the opposing team commits a minor violation, such as offside.

instep: The part of the foot covered by the shoelaces. The instep is used to make powerful kicks.

juggling: The technique of keeping the ball in the air by making touches with the feet, thighs, chest, and head. Juggling is a good way to improve ball control.

kick-in: In indoor soccer, the method of returning the ball into play after it goes out of bounds over a sideline. A player kicks from the spot where the ball went out of play.

kickoff: The way to begin play at the start of the game, after halftime, and after a goal is scored. The ball is played from the center spot and

goal area: The area immediately around the goal from which goal kicks are taken. The goal area measures 6 yards by 20 yards.

goalkeeper: One of a team's 11 players on the field. As the primary defender of the team's goal, the goalkeeper is the only player who can use his or her hands to play the ball (except for a throw-in).

goal kick: A free kick taken by the team defending the goal after the ball goes out of bounds and was last touched by the opposing team. The goal kick is taken from the goal area.

must rotate one full turn before it is touched by another player. During kickoff, opposing players must stay outside of the center circle.

major violation: A foul for which the opposing team is awarded a direct free kick. Major violations include handball, pushing, holding, and tripping.

marking: The technique of defending in which a player stays close to an opponent, guarding against an attack by the opponent.

midfielder: A position on the field between the forwards and the fullbacks. Midfielders must play both offense and defense.

minor violation: A foul for which the opposing team is awarded an indirect free kick. Minor violations include dangerous play, obstruction, and offside.

obstruction: A deliberate attempt to block an opponent's movement instead of playing the ball.

offside: A player is offside if he or she is on the opponents' half of the field with only one opponent between the player and the goal when the ball is played. Offside is a minor violation.

one-touch pass: A technique used to receive the ball and pass it on with only one touch.

passing: Playing the ball to a teammate by kicking or heading. Passing is one of the most important ways of moving the ball on the field.

penalty arc: The arc connected to the penalty area, outside of which players must stand during a penalty kick.

penalty area: The large area marked in front of each goal, which surrounds the goal area. The goalkeeper may use the hands to play the ball only within this area. If a major violation is committed within the penalty area by the defending team, the opposing team is awarded a penalty kick.

penalty kick: A direct free kick taken after a major violation is committed by the opponents in their own penalty area. The penalty kick is taken from the penalty spot.

penalty spot: The spot from which penalty kicks are taken. The penalty spot is located 12 yards in front of the center of the goal.

positioning: The technique used by a goalkeeper to block the goal from the opponent. By moving into certain positions in front of the goal, the goalie can cut off the angles open to a shooter.

punt: One of the ways a goalkeeper may put the ball into play after making a save. The goalie holds the ball out in front and makes an aerial kick with his or her laces. Punting enables the goalkeeper to send the ball far downfield.

red card: The referee's signal to inform a player that he or she is expelled from the game.

scissors kick: An aerial kick done while jumping up and backwards in a back somersault motion. Also called a **bicycle kick**.

shooting: An attempt to score a goal by kicking, heading, or otherwise touching the ball to send it toward the goal.

shot on goal: An attempt to score a goal that requires a save.

sliding tackle: An advanced defensive technique used to quickly take the ball away from an opponent by sliding.

support pass: A pass to a teammate positioned behind the passer.

tackle: A defensive technique used to take the ball away from an opponent.

throw-in: The method of returning the ball into play after it has been played out of bounds over the sideline by an opponent.

trapping: Coming into possession of the ball by collecting and controlling it.

volley pass: A one-touch pass made in the air.

wall pass: A one-touch pass made to the player from whom the ball was received.

wing: A player in the outside forward position.

yellow card: A referee's warning signal to a player to inform him or her that another misconduct will result in being expelled from the game.

FURTHER READING

Arnold, Caroline. *Soccer: From Neighborhood Play to the World Cup.* New York: Franklin Watts, 1991.

Chyzowych, Walter. *The Official Soccer Book.* Chicago, Illinois: Rand McNally & Company, 1978.

La Blanc, Michael and Richard Henshaw. *The World Encyclopedia of Soccer.* Detroit, Michigan: Gale Research, 1994.

Luxbacher, Joseph A. and Gene Klein. *The Soccer Goalkeeper.* Champaign, Illinois: Human Kinetics Publishers, 1993.

Morrison, Ian. *The Hamlyn Encyclopedia of Soccer.* London: The Hamlyn Publishing Group, Ltd., 1989.

Yannis, Alex. *Inside Soccer.* New York: McGraw-Hill, Inc., 1980.

FOR MORE INFORMATION

Intercollegiate Soccer Association of America
1821 Sunny Drive
St. Louis, MO 63122

United States Soccer Federation (USSF) National Office
1801-11 South Prairie Avenue
Chicago, IL 60616

United States Youth Soccer Association
899 Presidential Drive
Suite 117
Richardson, TX 75082

INDEX